BIG FUN 2

WORKBOOK

T0345689

Mario Herrera

Barbara Hojel

Big Fun
Workbook 2 with Audio CD

Pearson Education, 10 Bank Street, White Plains, NY 10606 USA

Staff credits: The people who made up the **Big Fun** team, representing editorial, production, design, manufacturing, and marketing, are Isabel Arnaud, Rhea Banker, Danielle Belfiore, Carol Brown, Kim Casey, Tracey Munz Cataldo, Dave Dickey, Gina DiLillo, Christine Edmonds, Erin Ferris, Nancy Flaggman, Yoko Mia Hirano, Penny Laporte, Christopher Leonowicz, Emily Lippincott, Maria Pia Marrella, Jennifer McAliney, Kate McLoughlin, Linda Moser, Kyoko Oinuma, Leslie Patterson, Sherri Pemberton, Salvador Pereira, Pamela Pia, Juan Carlos Portillo, Jennifer Raspiller, Aristeo Redondo, Nicole Santos, Susan Saslow, Kimberley Silver, Jane Townsend, Kenneth Volcjak, Lauren Weidenman, and Carmen Zavala.
Text composition: Isabel Arnaud
Illustration credits: A Corazón Abierto, Francisco Morales, Luis Alberto Montiel Villegas

Printed in USA
ISBN-10: 0-13-344522-4
ISBN-13: 978-0-13-344522-0
10 17

PEARSON ELT ON THE WEB

PearsonELT.com offers a wide range of classroom resources and professional development materials. Access course-specific websites, product information, and Pearson offices around the world.

Visit us at **www.pearsonELT.com**.

CONTENTS

1 My School 1

2 My Senses 11

3 My Family 21

4 My Toys 31

5 Food 41

6 My Clothes 51

7 Animals.................... 61

8 My World 71

9 Show Time! 81

BIG FUN
Song

Chorus

*From the sky to the ground
And all the way around—
We can have big fun!
If there's rain, if there's sun,
Let's play with everyone.
We can have big, big fun!*

**Take a walk outside.
Our world is big and wide.
There are flowers and trees
And yellow bumblebees.
Buzz, buzz, buzz!**

(Chorus)

**Join your hands with me.
Let's see what we can see!
Then take a closer look.
We'll learn beyond our book.
Look, oh, look!**

(Chorus)

1 MY SCHOOL

Find and circle.

Trace and color.

Vocabulary Practice: *shelves, book, scissors, marker*
Language Practice: *These are (scissors). This is (a book).*

Look and match.

Vocabulary Practice: *inside, outside; markers, hoops, jungle gym, scissors, ball, box, books*

Look and draw a ball in each scene. Color.

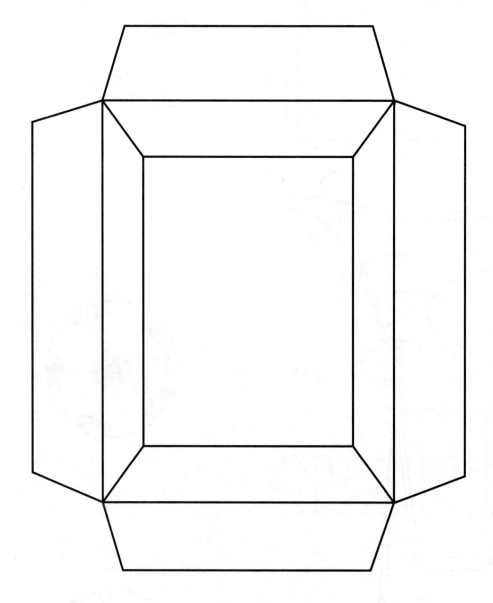

in the box

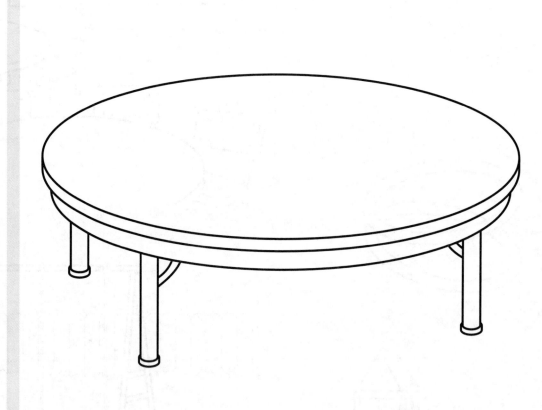

on the table

Vocabulary and Language Review: *in, on; ball, box, table*

Trace the shapes. Count and match.

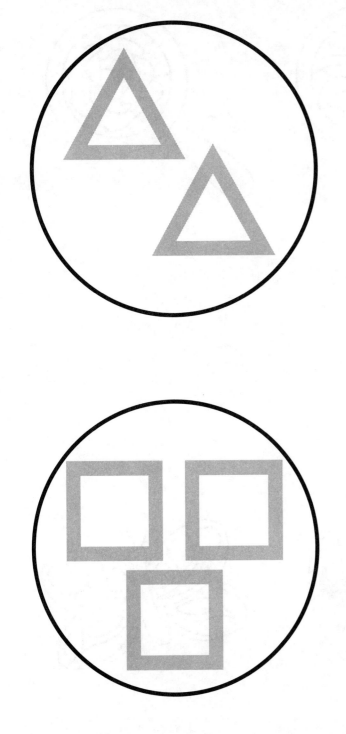

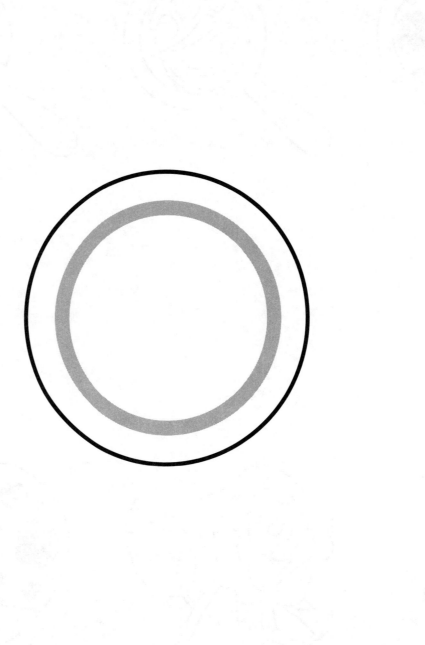

1

2

3

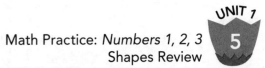

Look and match. Color.

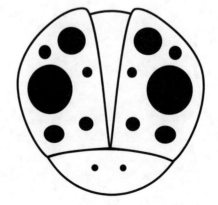

Pre-reading Practice: Identifying and matching for visual discrimination

Look and listen. Trace.

Draw and Color

Are they listening to the teacher?
Look and color the correct face.

Values: We respect the teacher and listen.

Trace the numbers and follow the trails.

Amazing: Science Connection: *snail, trail*

MY SCHOOL

Draw your school.

2 MY SENSES

Find and circle.

FIND IT: *banana (taste), bee (hear), ball (touch)*

Draw the missing body parts. Color.

Vocabulary Practice: *eyes, hands, nose, ears, tongue*

Circle or cross out.

Vocabulary Practice: *see, hear, smell, taste, touch*

Match and color.

Vocabulary Review: *touch, hear, see, smell, taste*

Trace and draw the shapes.

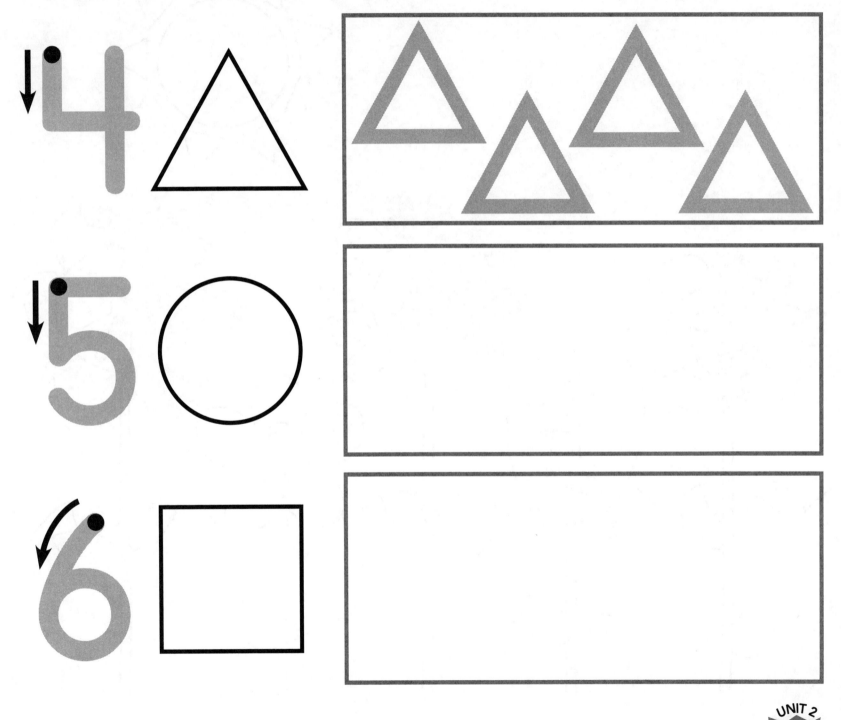

✂ **Cut out, match, and paste.**

Pre-reading Practice: Identifying and matching for visual discrimination
Phonics Practice: Initial Sound /s/

Look and listen. Draw the arrow to the next picture.

Guessing Game

Are they waiting for their turn?
Look and match.

Values: We are polite and wait for our turn.

Look and match.

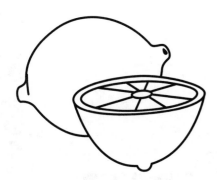   

Amazing: Science Connection: *tongue, taste buds*

MY SENSES

Draw something you can smell and something you can hear.

3 MY FAMILY

Find and circle.

FIND IT: *bird, doll, sandwich*

Trace and color.

Vocabulary Practice: *grandmother, grandfather, aunt, uncle*

Point and say. Draw a cousin or a pet.

Trace and draw or paste photos of family members.

Vocabulary Review: Family members; *house*

Connect the dots and color. Complete the number line.

1 2 3 _ 5 6 _ 8 _

✂ **Cut out, match, and paste.**

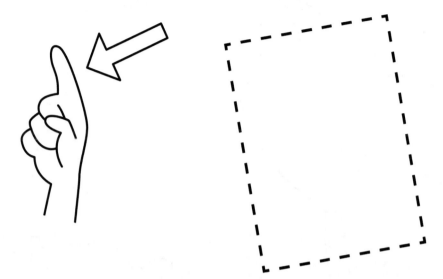

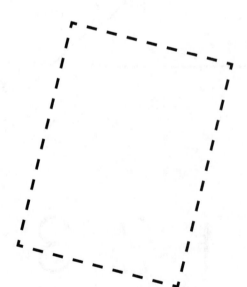

Look and listen. Draw an arrow to the next picture.

Show and Tell

Do they appreciate their family members? Look and color the correct face.

Values: We appreciate family members.

Trace, draw more eggs, and color.

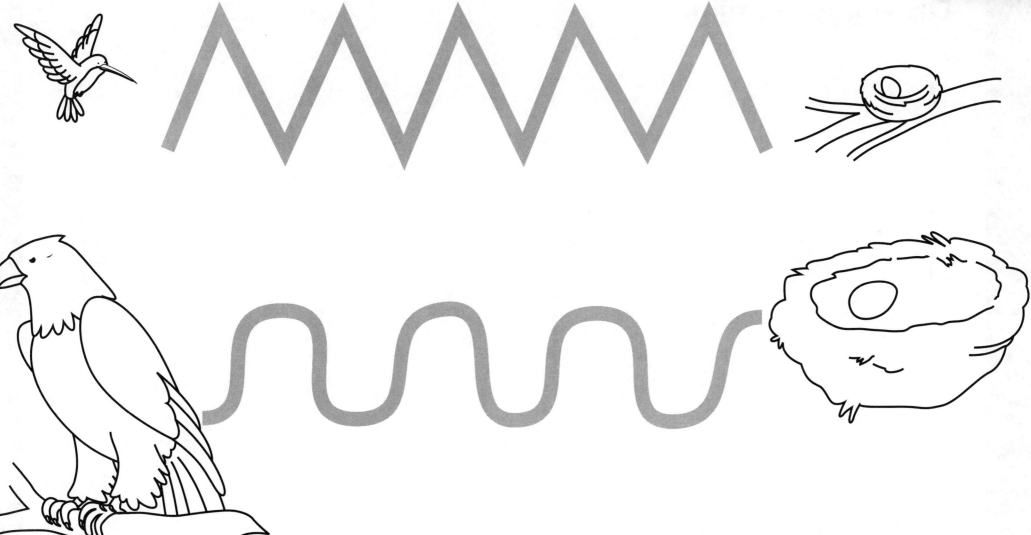

Amazing: Science Connection: *hummingbird, eagle, nest*

MY FAMILY

Draw your family.

Personal Response

4 MY TOYS

Find and circle.

FIND IT: *airplane, kite, ball*

Same or different? Color the frames if the pictures are the same.

Vocabulary Practice: *slide, swing, tricycle, car*

Circle a toy you have in blue. Then circle a toy you want in green.

I have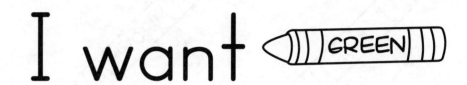

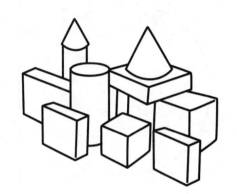

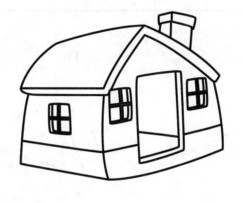

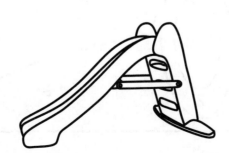

Vocabulary Practice: *blocks, action figure, play house, game, tricycle, slide*
Vocabulary Review: *doll, teddy bear*

Color the crayons. Then color by number.

1 BLUE

2 BROWN

3 YELLOW

4 RED

5 ORANGE

Vocabulary Review: *car, teddy bear*; colors; numbers

Count and circle.

10   11   12

10   11   12

Draw an animal and say the sound.

oo ahh

arf, arf

quack

Pre-reading Practice: Big and small animals help explain how letter names and sounds work.

Look and listen. Draw an arrow to the next picture.

Outdoor Fun

Are they sharing? Color the correct face.

VALUES

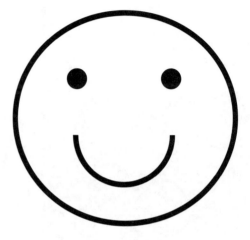

Values: We share to make something together.

Look. Circle or cross out.

I can see...

I can hear...

I can touch...

Amazing: Science Connection: *clouds, thunder, lightning, rain*

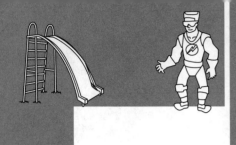

MY TOYS

Draw your toys.

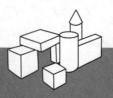

5 FOOD

Find and circle.

FIND IT: *carrot, cookie, apple*

Point and say. Draw food that you like.

Vocabulary Practice: *meat, fish, oranges, salad*

✂ Do you like…? Trace. Then cut out and paste.

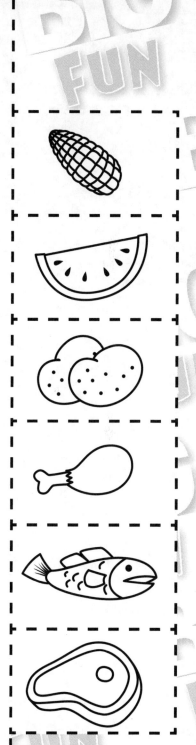

What do you want to eat? Choose a food or a drink in each section and circle.

Vocabulary Review: *salad, soup, chicken, meat, fish, milk, juice, watermelon, cookies*

Connect the dots. Then draw candles and color.

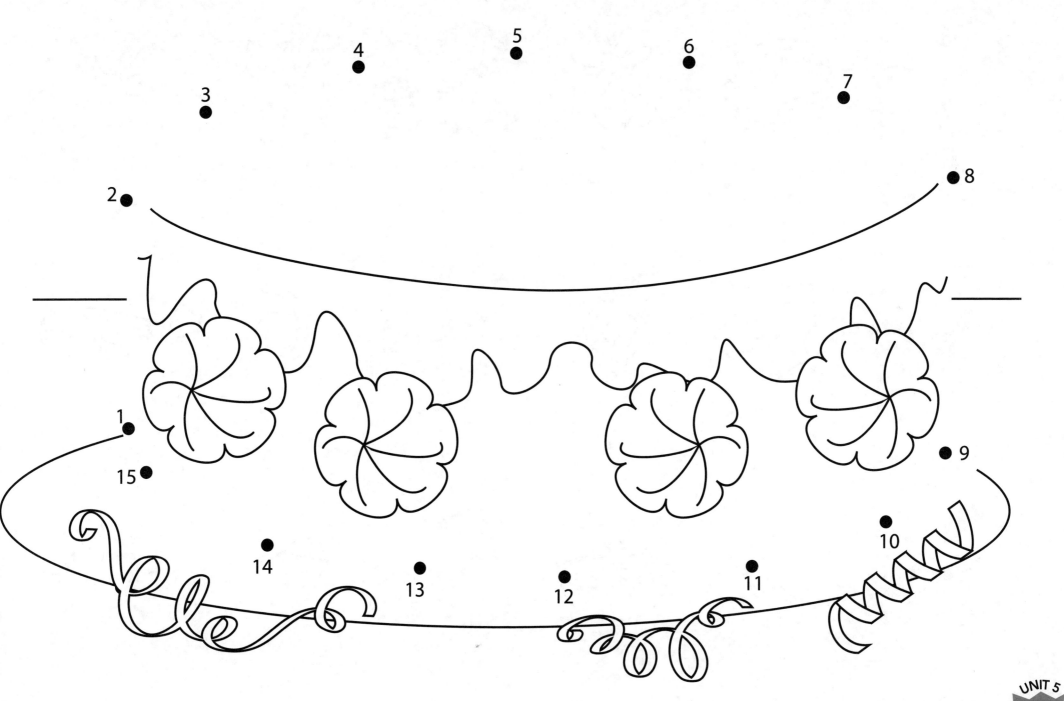

Trace. Circle the items that begin with /s/.

Pre-reading and Pre-writing Practice: *Ss*
Phonics Words: *sandwich, socks, soup, seal, six, sun*

Look and listen. Draw an arrow to the next picture.

I Like Apples

VALUES

Are they using table manners?
Look, trace, and draw a happy or a sad face.

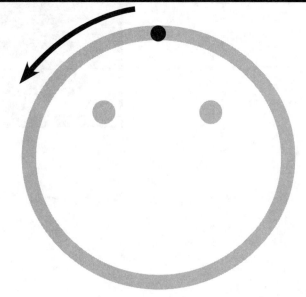

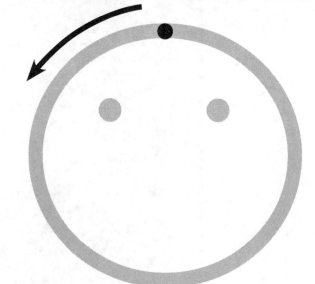

Values: We use table manners.

Color and paste orange tissue paper balls on the tree.

Amazing: Science Connection: *fruit, seeds*

FOOD

Draw your favorite food.

6 MY CLOTHES

Find and circle.

FIND IT: *socks, skirt, fish*

Color the crayons. Then trace and color by number.

1 GREEN 2 PINK 3 ORANGE 4 YELLOW 5 BLACK

Vocabulary Practice: *shorts, sandals, hat, bathing suit*

✂ **Cut out and paste the clothes.**

Vocabulary Practice: *umbrella, raincoat, boots, jacket*

Look and draw the weather.

Vocabulary Practice: *rainy, sunny*
Vocabulary Review: *raincoat, umbrella, hat, boots, bathing suit, shorts, sandals*

Count and draw one more. Trace.

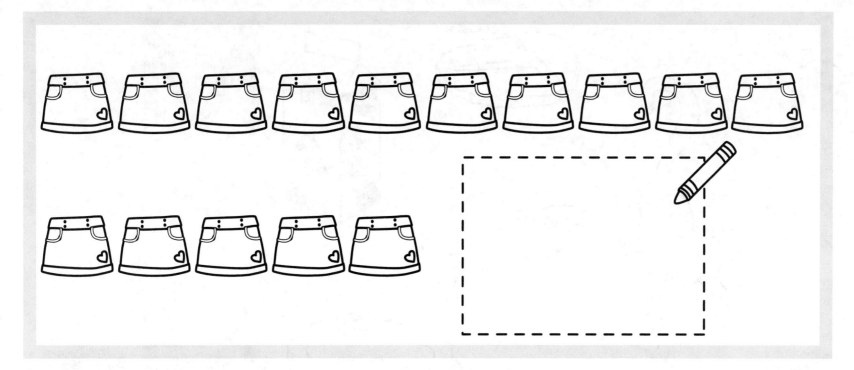

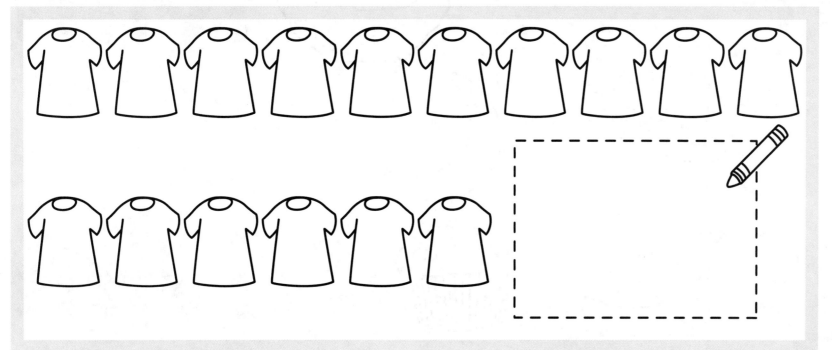

Trace and match with items that begin with /m/.

Pre-reading and Pre-writing Practice: *Mm*
Phonics Words: *monkey, meat, milk, moon, mouth, muffin*

Look and listen. Draw an arrow to the next picture.

How Many?

Who is helping? Look and match.

Values: We help others.

Color and paste brightly colored paper feathers.

Amazing: Science Connection: *parrot, feathers*

MY CLOTHES

Draw your favorite clothes.

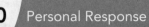

7 ANIMALS

Find and circle.

Match and color.

Vocabulary Practice: *rabbit, cow, sheep, chicken*

Draw a horse in the barn. Trace and color.

Vocabulary Practice: *barn, chicken, lamb, horse; in*

✂ **Cut out and paste two animals. Say.**

Vocabulary Review: *rabbit, chicken, cow, horse*
Language Practice: *This is a (rabbit). That is a (horse).*

Connect the dots and color. Draw yourself inside.

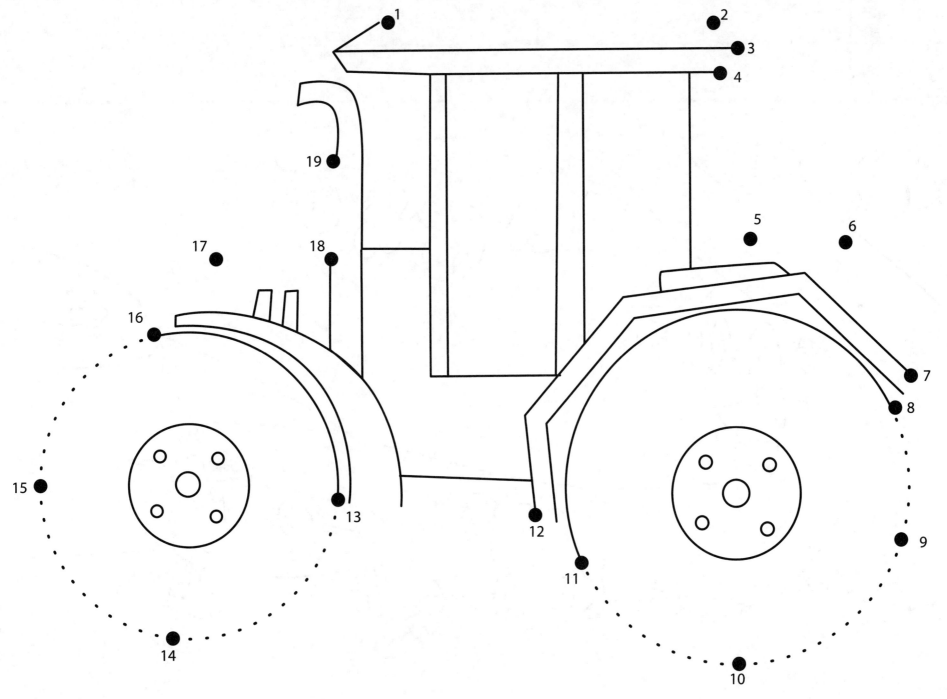

Math Practice: *Numbers 1–19*
Vocabulary Practice: *tractor*

Trace and write. Color things that begin with /l/.

Pre-reading and Pre-writing Practice: *Ll*
Phonics Words: *lemon, lion, lamb, leaves, lollipop, lemonade, lizard*

Look and listen. Draw an arrow to the next picture.

Where Are the Lambs?

Are they taking care of the animals? Color the correct face.

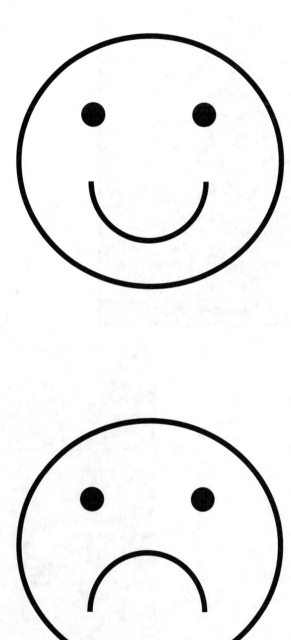

Values: We take care of animals.

Number, trace, and draw a chick in the broken eggshell.

Amazing: Science Connection: *egg, eggshell, chick*

ANIMALS

Draw your favorite farm animals.

8 MY WORLD

Find and circle.

Where are they? Look and match.

Vocabulary Practice: *restaurant, school, fire station, park*

✂ **Cut out and paste the places. Say.**

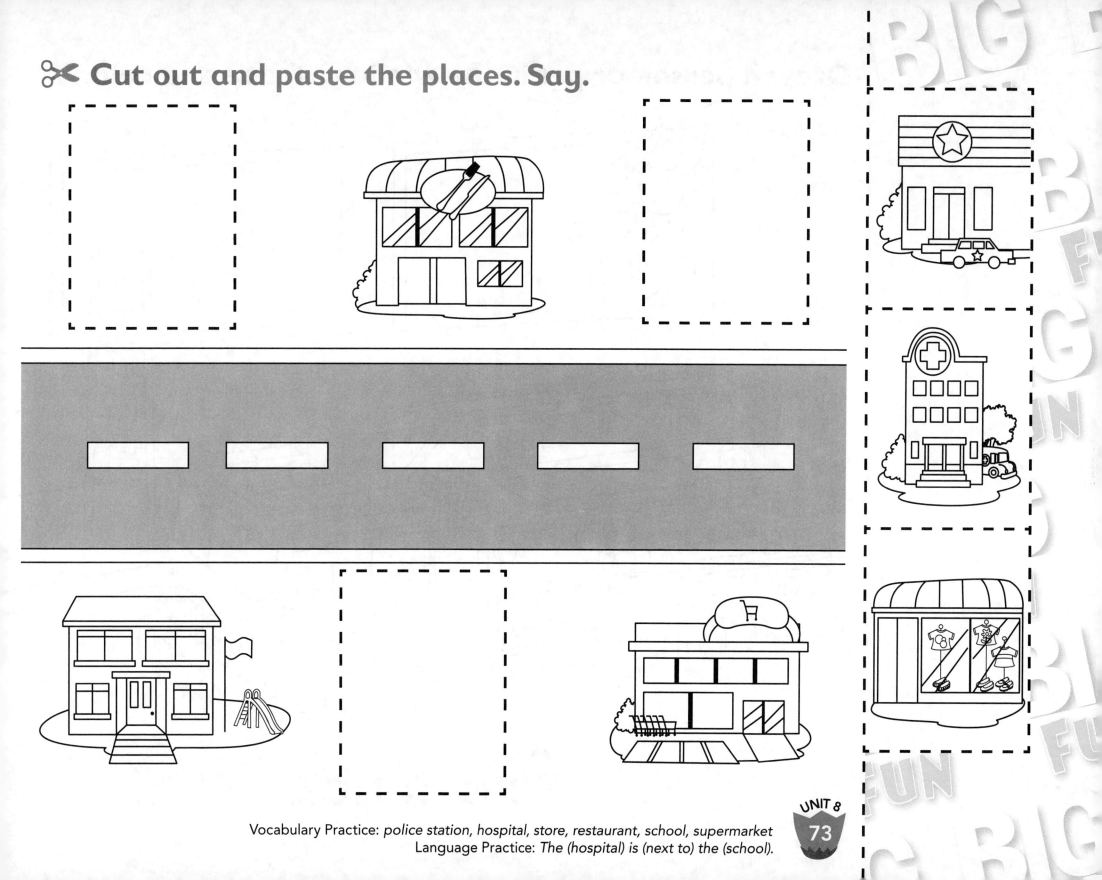

Vocabulary Practice: *police station, hospital, store, restaurant, school, supermarket*
Language Practice: *The (hospital) is (next to) the (school).*

Draw a person or pet in the window. Trace and color.

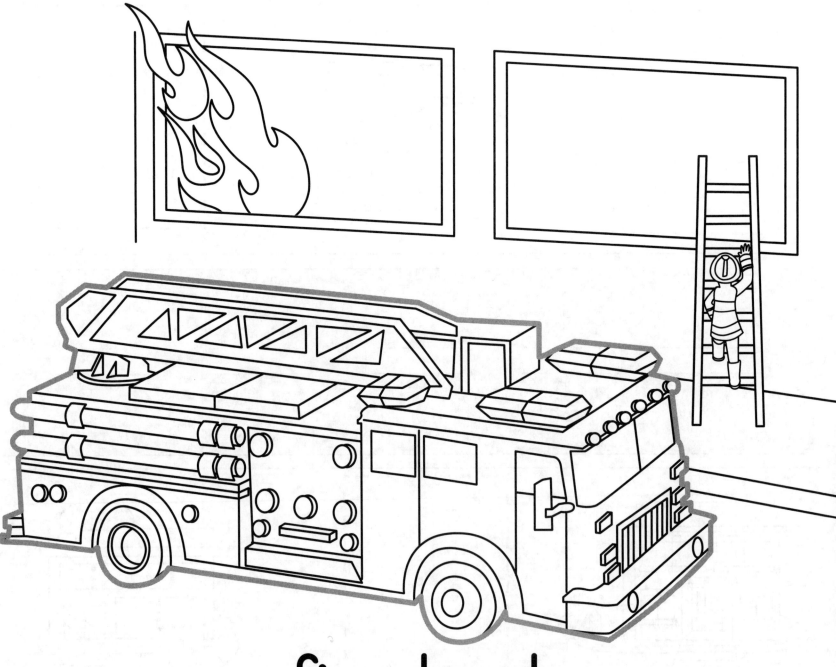

fire truck

Vocabulary Review: *fire truck, firefighter*

Count and color 20 bubbles. Complete the number line.

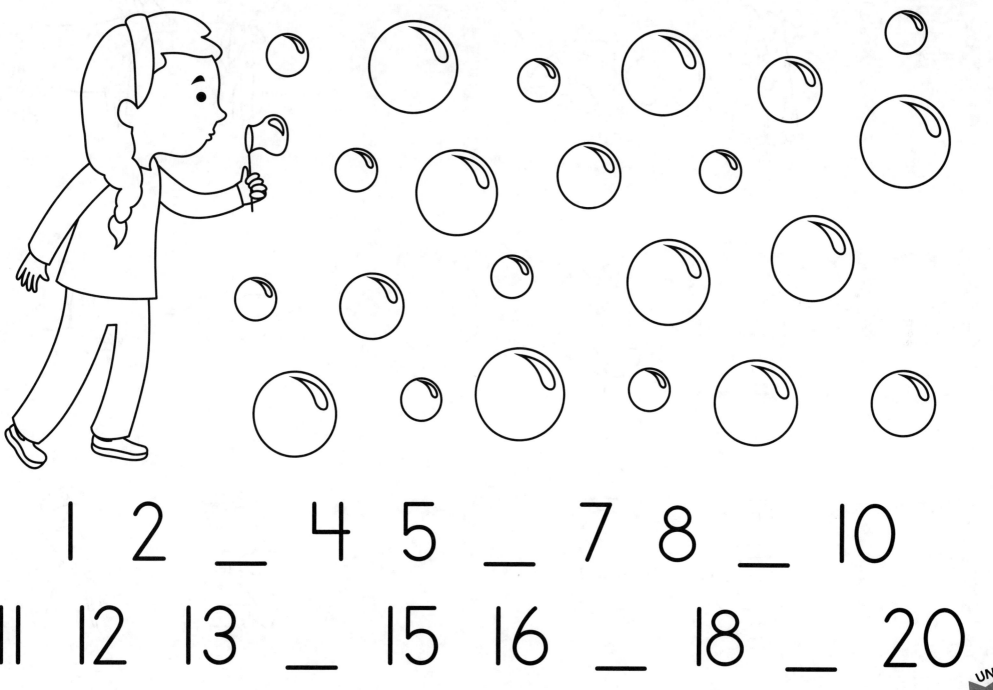

1 2 _ 4 5 _ 7 8 _ 10

11 12 13 _ 15 16 _ 18 _ 20

Trace. Circle the items that begin with /f/.

Pre-reading and Pre-writing Practice: *Ff*
Phonics Words: *fish, flower, five, farmer, feet, firefighter*

Look and listen. Draw an arrow to the next picture.

Shopping with Mommy

VALUES

Look and match.

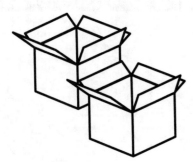

Values: We recycle.

Trace the moons. Draw a moon in the sky and color.

Amazing: Science Connection: *crescent moon, half moon, full moon, telescope*

MY WORLD

Draw your favorite place.

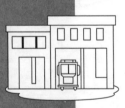

9 SHOW TIME!

Look and review.

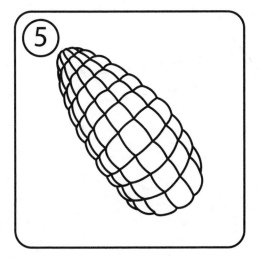

Review Units 1–8: *scissors, nose/smell, aunt/uncle/cousin, tricycle, corn, shorts, lamb/sheep, hospital*

Unit 1: Look and say. Color the objects you use inside a classroom.

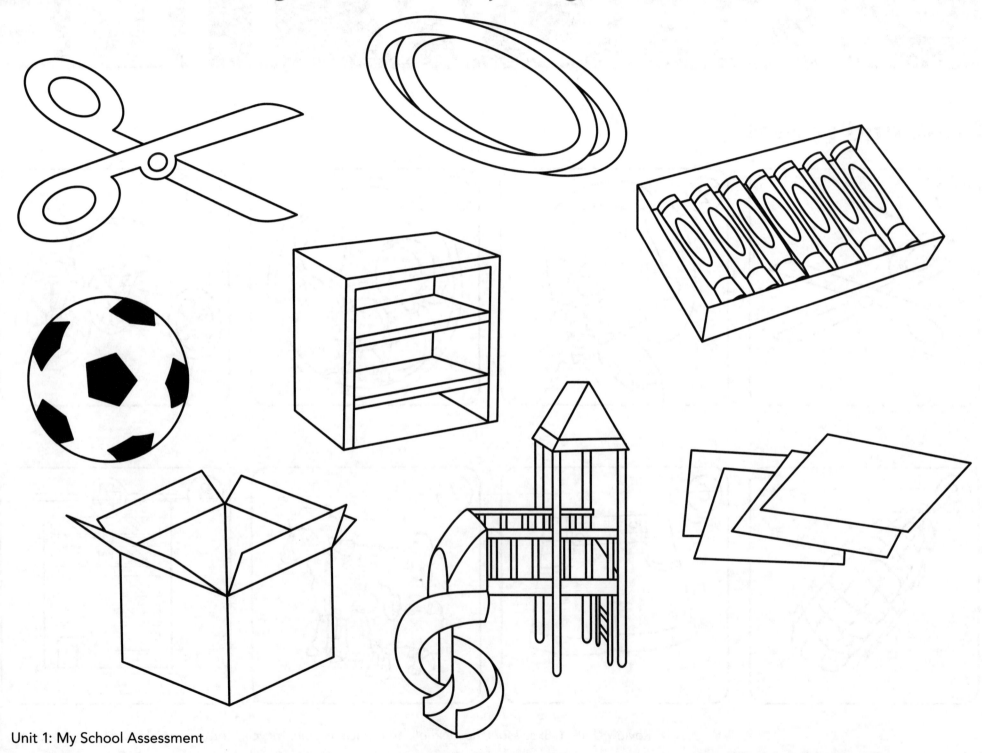

Unit 2: Look and match what you hear, smell, and taste.

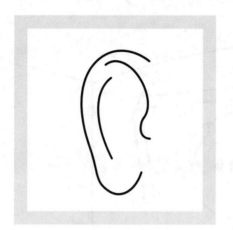

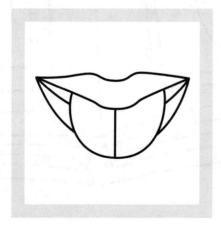

Unit 3: Name the family members and pets. Circle the type of home you live in.

Unit 4: What toys do you have? Look and circle.

Unit 5: What do you like? Look and complete the faces.

I like...

I don't like...

Unit 6: What is missing? Look and match.

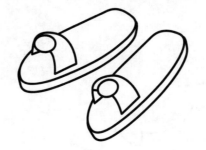

Unit 7: Where are the animals? Look and say.

Unit 7: Animals Assessment

Unit 8: Where is the...? Place a marker and say.

Workbook Audio CD

BIG FUN

WORKBOOK 2 Audio CD

TRACK	ACTIVITY
1	Copyright information
2	"Big Fun Theme Song"

Little Books

3	Unit 1 *Draw and Color*
4	Unit 2 *Guessing Game*
5	Unit 3 *Show and Tell*
6	Unit 4 *Outdoor Fun*
7	Unit 5 *I Like Apples*
8	Unit 6 *How Many?*
9	Unit 7 *Where Are the Lambs?*
10	Unit 8 *Shopping with Mommy*

Songs and Chants

Unit 1: My School

11	"Hello Song"
12	"Stop, Look, and Listen Chant"
13	"Let's Have Fun"
14	"Good-bye Song"
15	Target Song "My School"
16	"Look at Me Chant"
17	"Numbers 1, 2, 3 Chant"
18	"We Have Finished Chant"
19	"Amazing Snails Chant"

Unit 2: My Senses

20	Target Song "Senses"
21	"My Crayon Box"
22	"Numbers 4, 5, 6 Chant"
23	"Letter Sounds (S)"
24	"Taking Turns Chant"
25	"Amazing Tongues"

Unit 3: My Family

26	Target Song "My Family"
27	"People We Know"
28	"Numbers 7, 8, 9 Chant"
29	"Letter Sounds (*M* and *F*)"
30	"Grandma Gave Me Cookies"

Unit 4: My Toys

31	"Days of the Week"
32	"Actions Song"
33	Target Song "My Toys"
34	"Writing Numbers 10, 11, 12"
35	"Animals Talk"
36	"Sometimes"
37	"Amazing Clouds"

Unit 5: Food

38	Target Song "Food"
39	"Writing Numbers 13, 14, 15"
40	"Letter *S* Song"
41	"Being Polite Song"

Unit 6: My Clothes

42	Target Song "My Clothes"
43	"Put It On Chant"
44	"Writing Numbers 16, 17"
45	"Letter *M* Song"

Unit 7: Animals

46	Target Song "The Farm"
47	"This and That Song"
48	"Writing Numbers 18, 19"
49	"Letter *L* Song"

Unit 8: My World

50	"It's a Week Chant"
51	Target Song "My World"
52	"Writing Number 20"
53	"Prepositions Chant"
54	"Letter *F* Song"
55	"Shapes and Colors Song"
56	"Night Sky"

Unit 9: Show Time!

57	"Show Time"

has finished *Big Fun* **Workbook 2!**

Good job!